Dog Saves Duck

Written by **Julie Cantrell**

To Mesa, Bridger, & Sage —
Happy Reading!
Julie Cantrell

This book was written to celebrate all the unlikely animal friends and the people who love them.

Dog Saves Duck

Text and image copyright ©2022 by Julie Cantrell

Published by BlueSpark Press
an Imprint of BlueSpark Editorial
8050 Brookhollow West Drive #41183
Houston, TX. 77241 USA
Nov. 2022, First Edition

All Rights Reserved. No part of this book may be reproduced, stored in a retrieved system, or transmitted in any form or by any means—electronic, mechanical, photoshop, recording, or otherwise—without written permission of the author or publisher, except for brief quotations in reviews.
Distribution of digital editions of this book in any format via the internet or any other means without the author and publisher's written permission by license agreement is a violation of copyright law and is subject to substantial fines and penalties. Thank you for supporting the author's rights by purchasing only authorized editions.

Library of Congress Control Number: 2022915849

ISBN: 978-1-7377933-0-4

Written by Julie Cantrell
Design by Alison Tutton Robins
Photography by Robert Bradford and Julie Cantrell
Dog Saves Duck

Meet Dog.

Dog is big and white. He is very sweet and happy.

Every day, Dog goes fishing with his dad.

He loves to watch the ducks at the lake.

Meet Duck.

Duck is little and yellow.
She is very sweet and happy.

One day a bad storm began to blow over the lake.

The thunder roared.

The rain fell.

Duck lost her family. She was cold and wet and alone.

Duck cried.

The big white dog found the little yellow duck crying in the rain.

Dog looked all around the lake but he could not find Duck's family.

"Don't worry, Duck," said Dog. "I'll take care of you."

Dog carried Duck home to his warm, dry house.

There they met Dog's sister, the soft black cat.

"Who is this?" asked Cat.

"This is Duck," said Dog.

"Look! She has a black dot on her head just like you," said Cat.

Dog kept Duck safe and warm. **They snuggled.**

They played.

They swam.

(Can you point to the **black dots** on their heads?)

And they became best friends.

Every day,
Duck grew

bigger ...

And bigger ...

And bigger ...

She grew so big that her fluffy yellow feathers fell out.

New ones grew in, bright and white.

Surprise!

Now Duck and Dog were **BOTH** big and white with black dots on their heads. **They matched!**

After she had grown big and strong, Duck snuggled very close to Dog.

Duck said,

"Thank you for saving me from the storm.

Thank you for keeping me safe and warm.

Now I have a long beak to help me eat, fast legs to help me walk, webbed feet to help me swim, and wide wings to help me fly.

It is time for me to go live with other ducks."

So the big white duck
flew back to the lake.

Duck quickly made lots of duck friends.

And she was very happy.

Now Dog goes to visit Duck
at the lake every day.

They still snuggle.
They still play. They still swim.

The big white dog and the big white duck will be best friends forever.

Mr. Beaux Jangles ("Beau")
is the big white dog who rescued the little yellow duck during a torrential Texas downpour.

Dot
is the Muscovy duck who stole Beau's heart.

They really do match and they really are best friends.

Scootaloo ("Scoot")
is the soft black cat with an equally kind soul.

Julie Cantrell is a *New York Times* and *USA Today* bestselling author who has published books for all ages. A certified speech-language pathologist and literacy advocate, she now works full-time as a writer, editor, instructor, and public speaker.

Robert Bradford is an architect and avid fisherman who rescues animals of all kinds. He's also a photographer who captured many of the photos in this book.

Learn more at **www.juliecantrell.com** and sign up for a free monthly dose of joy and positivity.

See footage of **Dog and Duck** in action:

TikTok **@juliecantrellauthor**
Instagram **@juliecantrell**

CPSIA information can be obtained
at www.ICGtesting.com
Printed in the USA
JSHW041049280323
39234JS00003B/11